Princess Isabella
and
The Mystery of the
Disappearing Golf Balls

K.B. Lebsock & Jessica Wulf

Using a QR scanner app, place smart device
over QR codes to view bonus videos.

Princess Isabella
and
The Mystery of the Disappearing Golf Balls
by
K.B. Lebsock and Jessica Wulf

Joshua Tree Publishing
• Chicago •

JoshuaTreePublishing.com

ISBN: 978-1-941049-64-8

COPYRIGHT 2016 K.B. LEBSOCK & JESSICA WULF
All rights reserved. No part of this book may be reproduced or transmitted in any form or by any means, electronic or mechanical, including photocopying, recording, or by any information storage and retrieval system without written permission from the authors.

Photography: K. B. Lebsock

Music composed and performed by: Jacob Martin
Video Editing: Christopher Blair Maywhort
Princess Isabella's Video Voice: Kendall Maywhort

ACKOWLEDGEMENTS

Thank you to all who contributed to the making of this book:
Golf Club Salesman: Jason Brandt; Veterinarian: Dr. Stephanie Dodge;
Sadie the Squirrel: Tracy Marshall;
Media Team: Matt Kolding, Paul Kolding and Donny Legino;
Autograph Seeker: Aubree Lebsock;
President of the Tournament: Dale Douglass; Auto Salesman: Paul Stevens;
Doggie participants (and the names of their caregivers):
Chica (Sarah Gilsdorf); Beau, Mandy & Roxie (Donna Taylor);
Domino (Sandy Urbanic); Gracie (Kathleen Stiny);
Melody (Sue Cianfarani); and QT Bear (Karen Ann Allard);
The Highlands Ranch Golf Club;
The Links Golf Club;
and The Castle Pines Golf Club.

PRINCESS ISABELLA

Princess Isabella!
She's here for you ladies and fellas
She's got talent, and she's got cutes
Just you watch what Princess Isabella can do

This Princess knows how to break it down
She can spin and swerve and prance around
She feels the rhythm, gets with the flow
She's coordinated as her matching dresses and bows

Princess Isabella!
Prim and pretty from her tail to the tip of her smella
She's got talent, and she's got cutes
But that ain't all that Princess Isabella can do

She's got the smarts to match her looks
You can find the proof in her detective books
When she's not dancing, she's still on the move
Thinking through the puzzles and collecting clues

Princess Isabella!
If you've read her mystery novellas
You know some problems only cuteness can solve
That's when you need Princess
Isabella, the dog!!!

THE ALARM WENT OFF ! ! !

but Princess Isabella was already awake.
Today was the BIG DAY - - -
The International Doggie Golf Tournament ! ! !

She had been practicing for months at the golf course.

Then she would stop by the Pro Shop to see Jason.
He had advised her to purchase a new 5 iron,
so she did.
They were sure the new club would help her game.

Now it was was time to get ready and go ! ! !
SHE COULDN'T BE LATE, so she zipped along in her speedy red car to the International Doggie Golf Tournament.

Chica, Gracie, Mandy, Domino, Roxie, QT Bear, Beau and Melody were already at the golf course, eager for the tournament to begin in a few minutes.

BUT it couldn't begin without Princess Isabella ! ! !

WHERE WAS SHE?

Princess Isabella arrived at the golf course in plenty of time and got in her golf cart. Before she went to the first tee, she made
ONE QUICK STOP ...

. . . by the Pro Shop where the Tournament Trophy was displayed. She decided she would try as hard as she could to **WIN THAT TROPHY!!!**

Isabella's playing partner, Melody, chose the club she was going to use and... proceeded to the first tee to start her round.

On the next hole, Isabella's ball hung on the lip before rolling in. She made her birdie putt, which was verified by Mr. Dale Douglass, the Tournament President. Then Isabella moved into the lead ! ! !

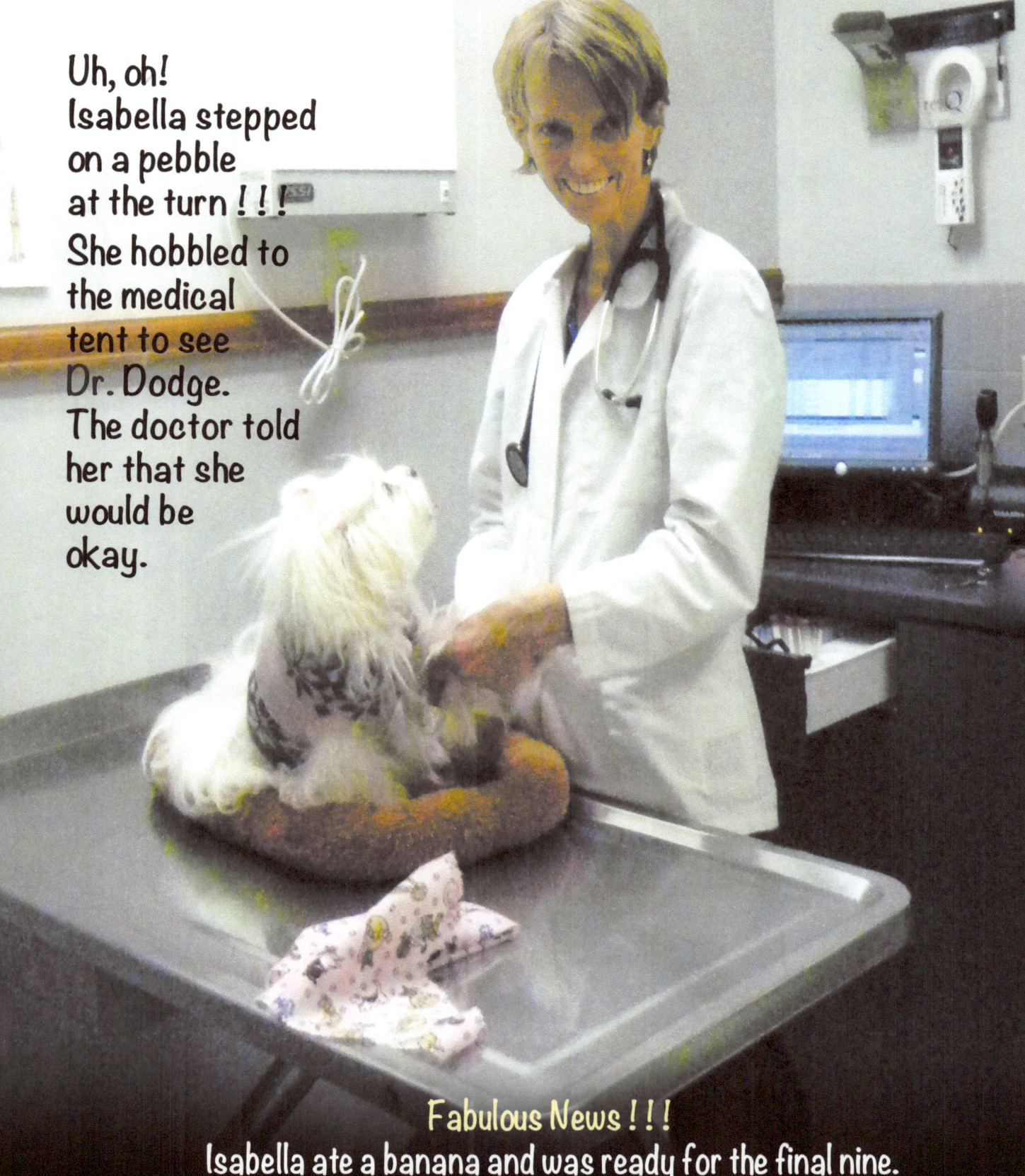

At that point, there were nine top contenders
in the International Doggie Golf Tournament ! ! !

Melody

Beau

QT Bear

Chica

Gracie

Mandy

Domino

Roxie

Isabella

A sudden storm came up, forcing a rain delay. While they waited it out, the doggies discussed the fact that a lot of their golf balls

had GONE MISSING ! ! !

When the tournament resumed, golf balls continued to disappear!!!

Isabella had a NEW MYSTERY TO SOLVE!!!

Uh, Oh!!!

QT Bear saw Princess Isabella talking to ...
Ummmm, something very strange.
What could that be?
QT Bear decided to just sit and wait
a bit for Isabella
to come back to the golf cart
and explain.

The squirrel scampered behind some bushes, then ran to a tree. Isabella did not want to scare the squirrel and make her run up the tree.
She asked the squirrel what her name was.
The answer was Sadie.

Isabella asked Sadie very gently why she was taking the golf balls.
"Golf balls?" Sadie asked, genuinely surprised.
"Aren't these a new kind of nut? They are so white and pretty ! ! !"
Isabella explained that the golf balls were not nuts at all and they would taste very awful if Sadie tried to eat one! She also explained that the Tournament players needed their golf balls so they could finish their game.

NOW SADIE FELT AWFUL!

She didn't mean to cause any trouble.

With a promise to bring all the golf balls back to the doggies,

SHE HURRIED OFF.

Princess Isabella reported to her friends what had happened. The doggies realized that now Sadie would not have any nuts to eat after she had gone to all that work to collect the golf balls. They decided to thank her for returning the golf balls by giving her 2 baskets of nuts in exchange. There she was!

They all met on the 10th fairway. True to her word, Sadie brought 2 baskets of golf balls to the doggies,

and she was delighted to get the 2 baskets of nuts. She thanked the doggies—then took her 2 baskets and

scampered away ! ! !

Now that the Mystery of the Disappearing Golf Balls had been solved, the doggies could once again focus on the Golf Tournament. Isabella checked the leader board and was happy to see that she was still leading the Tournament ! ! !

Princess Isabella was greeted by Paul, the President of Isabella's Fan Club. She was also interviewed by Don from Radio News, and photographed by Matt from the Doggie Press.
WHAT AN EXCITING FINISH ON THE 18TH HOLE ! ! !

Princess Isabella posed for pictures with Mr. Dale Douglass, the president of the Doggie International Golf Tournament. He presented her with the trophy. Isabella expressed that it was a tough tournament, and she loved every minute of it!

Isabella thought about all that had happened that day, and she realized that she had learned something

NEW AND IMPORTANT.

If one has a dream, a goal, and
works hard for it,
even if one runs into obstacles, like
Sadie the Squirrel mistaking
the golf balls
for nuts,
if one sticks with it and perseveres,
the goal can be met,

AND THE

DREAM

CAN

COME

TRUE !!!

Other Princess Isabella Adventures

Princess Isabella
and
The Mystery of the Pink Dragon

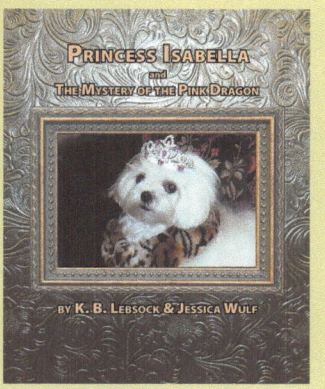

From her birthplace in Wyoming to her forever-home in Colorado, Princess Isabella leads a seemingly charmed life with people and friends who adore her. Then her happy life gets even better when she discovers in her doggie bed a new friend. Isabella and Pink Dragon soon become Best Friends. They go everywhere together and each night they snuggle under the froggie blanket to sleep. But then one day something mysterious and terrible happens: Pink Dragon disappears. And so begins Isabella's search for her dear friend.

ISBN: 978-0-9886577-7-9

Princess Isabella
and
The Mystery of the Golden Keys

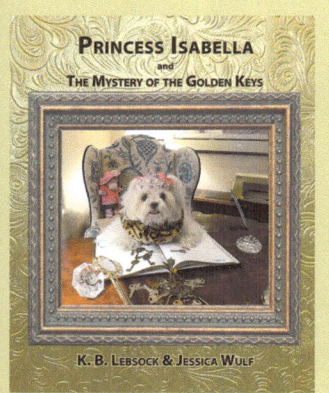

The day starts off normally for Princess Isabella when she goes to school to register and pick up her class assignments for the new school year. But then something strange happens: her teacher and all of her classmates each give her a mysterious Golden Key, with the puzzling message that she will one day know what all those keys are for and that she must be patient. Well, Princess Isabella isn't always good at being patient, especially when there is a mystery to solve! And so she sets off on the search for the meaning of the Golden Keys.

ISBN: 978-1-941049-01-3

www.ingramcontent.com/pod-product-compliance
Lightning Source LLC
Chambersburg PA
CBHW050756110526
44588CB00002B/24